Balkan Comfort Food
HOME COOKING FROM **THE HEART**
By Jas Brechtl

With love and gratitude I dedicate this book to:

My precious granddaughters, Avelyn (4) and Alyvia (1), who enjoy grandma's cooking and are always willing to assist in the kitchen. You add dashes of the perfect spices and heaps of sweetness to my life. Grandma loves you to the moon and back!

To all generations whose roots began in this unique and beautiful region with exceptional culinary customs: I hope this book will save some of your favorite recipes from falling into oblivion.

Acknowledgments

To my daughter Andrea, the light of my life, my biggest but fairest critic:
Thank you for your honesty, humor, friendship, and for always correcting my grammar. But most of all, thank you for making me a grandma. Mama loves you more than you know.

To my husband Robert, my favorite taste-tester and my rock who loves my broken English ["it's unique and it's what makes you-you"]:
Thank you for always encouraging me to reach my limits. I love you today.

To my dear friend who had a brilliant idea for my name-brand and to all of you who took time to help me with this book:
Thank you from the bottom of my heart. You know who you are.

To my All that's Jas fans:
Thank you for your loyalty and support.

Contents

Traditional Balkan food is like film photography. It might be slow and grainy but the finished product is authentic with a burst of flavors and an immense satisfaction. Today's food reminds me of digital photography. The meals are quick, made by blending layers and adding filters of ingredients that seemingly don't belong together. We are in a constant rush and have forgotten how to enjoy spending time in our kitchen lab, developing that special dish.

With this book, I'm dusting off old recipes and preserving the art of creating dishes that many generations before me have enjoyed. You'll find these pages filled with nostalgia, smells, and tastes of my childhood. I am displaced from the Balkans but my heart is still there, hidden in the fog of mountain tops and gliding atop the mist of green rivers.

I'm from the country with green pastures, poplar groves, snowcapped mountains with winding rivers, and stunning shorelines. I grew up in a red brick house with shutters the color of land's end. Rain mist in a dawn of spring and the scent of dry sage can carry me back to the boxwood abutted street and laughter in the evenings of the full moon.

I dream of my grandmother's wood stove where she fried freshly laid eggs in pork lard, of the world where you kiss the kids on top of their heads, and where all girls named Jas are pretty but lazy, so they told me. I come from a place where hearts are big and hugs are bigger, voices are loud, and smiles go twice around the ears.

I am Jas, a Bosnian expat living in Northern Indiana since the summer of 1998 following a six-year exile in Germany.

I was born way back in the winter of 1965. I grew up in a traditional European family, the kind of family that sits together for big weekend lunches. Those lunches always began with some kind of soup. It isn't a big lunch unless you begin it with a spoon.

In the early years of my life food never had a central position. It wasn't until much later that I learned to appreciate a good dish. I actually hated eating and hated helping in the kitchen. Cut the onions; peel the potatoes; stir the pot, etc. were unpopular chores ordered by my mom (who is an excellent cook, by the way) but while doing them I picked up the basic knowledge for food preparation.

I'm enthused by the freedom of substituting ingredients and experimenting with them that cooking allows you. And unlike my mother, I do not like any help (except my granddaughters'). Stay out of my kitchen while I'm cooking, but you're welcome to clean it afterward!

I have rounded up/down the weight and temperatures in conversion from imperial to metric system, respectively, simply because of how it is being used.

For example: 1lb of meat is 454g but where metric is used it would be sold/packaged in kilos. Half a kilo is 500g. By the same token, if the recipe calls for 500g of meat you wouldn't buy 1.1lb.

- I use a cup that measures 8oz/250ml. For dry ingredients like flour or sugar, the cup is always leveled.
- Oven temperatures vary. Please keep your eye on it during the last 10-15 minutes of baking.
- A stick of butter is 4oz/113.4g
- A tablespoon of butter is 0.5oz/14.2g
- Vegeta is made in Croatia by the Podravka Company, which describes it as an all-purpose seasoning made from a special blend of the finest vegetables, herbs, spices, and selected natural ingredients. I use it often instead of salt for soups, stews and meats. It is easily available in the US.
- Unless otherwise noted, any mention of sugar means granulated (white).
- Powdered sugar is also called confectioners' or icing sugar.
- If you want to use dried herbs instead of fresh, use half the amount.
- Unless otherwise noted, an onion is a medium-size yellow onion.
- Green onions are scallions or spring onions.
- I cook with grapeseed oil and olive oil, but you can use any oil you prefer unless it's specified.
- Tomato paste is also called tomato mark.
- Peppers are also known as capsicum.
- Coconut flour I use has a coarse texture, like cornmeal, but fine coconut flour can be used as well. Do not substitute with shredded coconut.
- For all other questions, feel free to email me at: allthatsjas1@gmail.com

Soups and Stews

BEAN SOUP WITH SMOKED MEAT - GRAH

Any type of smoked meat or sausage is good for this soup but smoked rib meat and bacon is traditional and yields the best flavor. Omit meat for the vegetarian version, serve with hearty bread and you'll still have a tasty and filling meal. It's like a hug in a bowl and it tastes best the next day. Serve with bread and salad of choice.

Serves 6-8

Ingredients:

1 lbs/500g dried beans (pinto, cranberry, navy or mixed beans)
1 teaspoon baking soda
3qt/3L cold water
1 lbs/500g smoked meat or smoked sausage
1 large onion, chopped
1 large carrot, sliced
½ green bell pepper, chopped
1 tomato, chopped
2 garlic cloves, minced
2 tablespoons fresh or dried parsley
2 bay leaves
1 tablespoon paprika
1 tablespoon black pepper
Salt or Vegeta to taste
¼ cup Oil
1 tablespoon all-purpose flour
1 teaspoon tomato paste

Directions:

In a large saucepan or Dutch oven add the rinsed and picked-over beans, baking soda and just enough water to cover. Bring to a boil, reduce the heat and cook for 15 minutes. Baking soda will soften the beans and help digest them.

Drain the beans and rinse. Return the beans to a clean pan. Add cold water and smoked meat, cover and bring to a boil. Reduce the heat and cook for 30 minutes. Add vegetables and spices. Return to a boil, reduce the heat and simmer, partially covered, for 1 to 2 hours or until beans and meat are done. Add water, as needed, while cooking, stirring occasionally.

To thicken the soup, heat the oil in a small frying pan over medium heat. Add flour. With a wooden spoon or a whisk continue to stir flour over low heat until flour is golden in color. Do not burn it! Add tomato paste and stir to combine. Pour the roux into the soup; stir and simmer for 10 minutes. Check soup for seasoning.

To me, nothing smells more like childhood than this simple and abundantly tasty beef soup. It is packed with vegetable flavors and loaded with semolina dumplings, my favorite soup garniture. I sometimes add noodles or rice instead of dumplings. It is delicious either way. Here is what you need for a pot full of comfort:

Serves 4-6

Ingredients:

For Beef Stock
1 onion
3 quarts/3l (about) water
2 tablespoons vegetable oil
1-2 beef shanks, marrow beef bone or other beef cut for soup
2-3 carrots
1 celery stalk, piece of celery root or a bunch of celery leaves
2 parsley roots or a bunch of parsley leaves
5-8 black peppercorns
1 cup cauliflower florets
Salt, Vegeta or beef bouillon to taste

For Semolina Dumplings
1 egg
2 tablespoons all-purpose flour
¼ teaspoon baking powder
½ cup cream of wheat
1 tablespoon salted butter, softened

Directions:

Beef Stock
Peel onion and cut in half. Place on a stove burner cut side down and brown on medium-high heat until almost charred. For gas stoves, place the onion in an ungreased frying pan and increase the heat to high.

Add onion and the rest of ingredients, except cauliflower and salt, to a large pot with water and bring to a boil. Lower the heat and simmer, covered, for a couple of hours or until meat is tender.
Strain the stock into a medium-sized pot, add cauliflower florets and salt. Bring to a simmer. When cauliflower is cooked, add dumplings.

Semolina Dumplings
In a small bowl, mix butter and egg with a fork. Combine flour and baking powder and stir into the egg mixture. The mixture will be soft. Add cream of wheat and mix until combined. Do not compress the mixture or your dumplings will be too hard.

Form dumplings by scooping out the mixture with a small spoon. Drop the dumplings into simmering soup. Return strained (whole or chopped) carrots and beef to the soup. Dumplings are cooked when they float back to the surface, in about 5-7 minutes.

Note: Do not make dumplings ahead of time or they will dry out. Dumplings will triple in size, so do not use large spoons to form them.

BEEF STEW – GOVEDJI SAFT

You don't need fancy ingredients to make a tasty stew. Simmering it long is the key. It allows the flavors plenty of time to develop. This beef stew is great by itself but do spoon it over potatoes or egg noodles.

Serves 4-6

Ingredients:

2 tablespoons oil
2lbs/1kg stew beef (or beef chuck cut into 2-inch pieces)
2 large onions, chopped
1 clove garlic, minced
2 bay leaves
1 large carrot, sliced
2 teaspoons salt
1 teaspoon freshly ground black pepper
1 teaspoon smoked paprika
1 tablespoon all-purpose flour
2 cups water
2 tablespoons tomato paste
½ cup tomato sauce

Directions:

Heat the oil in a large pot or Dutch oven over medium-high heat. Add meat to the pot and cook, stirring occasionally until browned all over, about 5-10 minutes. Searing meat cubes like this is a key to creating the kind of rich, caramelized flavors that make stews irresistibly good.

Add onions, garlic, carrots, and bay leaves. Season it with salt, freshly ground black pepper, and paprika. Cook, stirring occasionally until vegetables are softened and just starting to brown, about five minutes.

Sprinkle in the flour and cook until the raw flavor has cooked off, about two minutes. Pour in the water and tomato paste, scrape any browned bits from the bottom of the pot and increase the heat to bring to a boil. Add tomato sauce and immediately reduce the heat to low and simmer, stirring occasionally until the meat is knife tender, about 1 1/2 to 2 hours. Remove and discard the bay leaves before serving.

BOSNIAN CABBAGE STEW – BOSANSKI LONAC

Nourish your body and soul with this traditional no-stir dish packed with flavors. Layers of meat and vegetables are best cooked in a clay pot or Dutch oven, but any large pot you have on hand will do.

Serves 4-6

Ingredients:

2 tablespoons oil
1 large onion, diced
1 bell pepper, chopped
2 large carrots, sliced
1 garlic clove, minced
2 bay leaves
1 tablespoon tomato paste
2 tablespoons chopped fresh parsley
1 teaspoon black peppercorns
1 tablespoon paprika
1lb/500g mix of beef and pork stew meat
Salt and pepper to taste
1 large potato, diced
1 small cabbage head, cored and coarsely chopped
1 large tomato, diced
2 cups water, plus more if needed

Directions:

Drizzle the bottom of a large pot or Dutch oven with two tablespoons of oil. Place onions in the pot and add peppers, carrots, garlic, bay leaves, tomato paste, parsley, and peppercorns. Sprinkle with paprika.

Top with meat cubes and season with salt and pepper. Add potatoes and cabbage then top with chopped tomato. Don't worry if your pot is full to the top - the cabbage will cook down.

Cover and simmer on medium heat for 30 minutes then add two cups of water or beef broth. Lower the heat and cook for additional 1 ½ hours or until meat is tender. Stir before serving.

BROWN ROUX SOUP – AJNPREN SUPA

Roux soup requires just a handful of ingredients and it's cooked in no time. Making a meal out of next to nothing was my mom's best skill. She would ladle it over chunks of stale bread to add substance and save on food waste. Top with croutons and a dollop of sour cream to lift this soup from rags to riches.

Serves 3-4

Ingredients:

½ cup oil
1/3 cup all-purpose flour
2 teaspoons paprika
½ teaspoon caraway seeds (optional)
4 cups water
3 teaspoons Vegeta (substitute with a vegetable bouillon cube)
Salt and pepper to taste
To serve: croutons and sour cream

Directions:

Heat the oil in a medium-size pot. Stir in the flour. With a wooden spoon or a whisk continue to stir flour over low heat until flour is golden in color. Do not burn it!

Mix in paprika and caraway seeds, if using. Slowly add water or broth continuing to stir as it thickens. Season the soup with Vegeta or bouillon. Simmer the soup, stirring frequently for 15-20 minutes. Season it with salt and pepper to taste.

FISH STEW - BRODET

Fish stew (brodet) has emerged as a popular meal in rural slum areas; prepared from the leftover small and unattractive fish that fisherman couldn't sell. For a good brodet, you should have at least three kinds of fish.

Serves 4-6

Ingredients:

2lbs/1kg fish filets (preferably various salt-water fish)
Salt and pepper to taste
1 lemon, juiced
6 tablespoons olive oil
2 onions, chopped
2 garlic cloves, minced
1 bay leaf
2-3 large tomatoes, chopped
1 cup dry white wine
1 tablespoon fresh parsley leaves

Directions:

Rinse the fish and cut into pieces, about 2"/5cm in size. Place into a medium size bowl, season with salt and pepper, and add lemon juice; let sit.

Meanwhile, heat the olive oil in a skillet, Dutch oven or a large pot with a low rim. Add onions and sauté until soft. Add garlic, bay leaf and tomatoes and cook for 10-15 minutes.

Add fish and wine. Cook covered on low heat for 20-30 minutes. Do not stir while cooking, just shake the whole pot from time to time, or the fish will fall apart. Remove the bay leaf and sprinkle with parsley before serving. Adjust seasoning if necessary.

Serve the stew over corn mush/polenta or mashed potatoes.

OKRA WITH BEEF AND LAMB - BAMIJA

To fully enjoy the flavors of this hearty okra stew, serve it with crusty bread. Pour over rice to increase the serving amount. If using fresh okra, look for smaller, green pods and then rinse in water-vinegar mixture before cooking. Frozen okra doesn't need to be washed or thawed.

Serves 4-6

Ingredients:

3 tablespoon olive oil
1 large onion, chopped
1lb/500g beef for stew, cut into cubes
½ lb/250g lamb for stew, cut into cubes (can use ground lamb)
2 garlic cloves, minced
2 cups canned crushed tomatoes
4 cups water
1/8 teaspoon allspice
1/8 teaspoon nutmeg
1 bay leaf
Salt and pepper to taste
1lb/500g frozen okra
1 tablespoon lemon juice

Directions:

In a large pot, heat the olive oil over medium heat. Stir in onions and sauté until soft but not browned, about 5 minutes.

Add beef, lamb, and garlic and cook until liquid has evaporated and meat is browned. Stir in tomato sauce, water, and spices. Bring to a boil. Cover and simmer on low heat, stirring occasionally for 45-60 minutes or until meat is tender. If necessary, add more water.

Gently stir in frozen okra; sprinkle with lemon juice. Cook without stirring 20 minutes longer or until okra is cooked through and liquid has thickened. Taste for seasoning.

PORK STEW – SAFT OD SVINJETINE

The pickled pepper in pork stew adds a unique flavor to the dish. It's a match made in pork heaven. Serve over noodles, rice, mashed potatoes, boiled potatoes, baked potatoes or gnocchi and sprinkle with fresh parsley.

Serves 4

Ingredients:

2 large onions
3 tablespoons oil
1 yellow or red bell pepper, chopped
2 dry bay leaves
1lb/500g cubed pork stew meat
1 pickled or roasted pepper out of a jar
Salt and black pepper to taste
1 teaspoon concentrated tomato paste
1 tablespoon flour
2 tablespoons fresh parsley

Directions:

Sauté onions in oil, over medium heat for 5 minutes or until they are soft but not browned. Add bell pepper, bay leaves, and pork cubes to the pot. Stir all together, lower the heat, cover, and cook for 30 minutes, stirring occasionally.

Stir in sliced pickled pepper and season with salt and pepper to taste. Simmer on low heat for 45 minutes or until meat is tender.

Mix a tablespoon of flour with two tablespoons of water until smooth and pour it into the pot. Add tomato paste, stir and let simmer until the sauce thickens for about 15 minutes.

Growing up, stews and soups were on our menu during the weekdays like this easy one-pot potato and chicken goulash. Serve with a dollop of sour cream and alongside bread to scoop up the juices.

Serves 2

Ingredients:

2 tablespoons oil
1 onion, chopped
1 celery stalk, chopped
1 carrot, sliced
½ bell pepper, chopped
Black peppercorns (about ½ teaspoon)
2 bay leaves
2 serving-size chicken pieces, like thighs or drumsticks
1 tomato, chopped
1 garlic clove, minced
2 cups chicken stock
3 medium-size potatoes, peeled and quartered
1 teaspoon paprika
1 tablespoon fresh, chopped parsley (or 1 teaspoon dried)
Salt & pepper to taste
Sour cream (optional)

Directions:

In a pan, heat oil over medium-high heat.

Sauté onions, celery, carrots, peppers, peppercorns, and bay leaves until softened, about 5 minutes.
Add chicken, tomato, and garlic, and cook until chicken is no longer pink.

Add stock, potatoes, paprika and parsley and cook for 20 minutes or until potatoes are cooked. Add water if necessary, depending how thick you like your stews. Season stew with salt and pepper to taste.

SAUERKRAUT – KISELI KUPUS

Once served primarily as a winter dish, when large amounts of cabbage were finely cut and stored for fermentation, simmered sauerkraut with bacon and sausage is nowadays often found on our table regardless of the season. It's the best comfort food there is.

Serves 4

Ingredients:

2 tablespoons oil
4oz/100g bacon, sliced into pieces
1 onion, diced
1lb/500g smoked sausage, sliced
1lb/500g sauerkraut, rinsed and drained
1 clove garlic, minced
1 large bay leaf
½ teaspoon paprika
¼ teaspoon pepper
1/8 teaspoon salt
Water

Directions:

In a large skillet, saucepan or Dutch oven, heat the oil over medium-high heat. Add the bacon and onions; cook until bacon is almost crisp and onions are soft, about 10-15 minutes. Add sausage slices and cook until sausage begins to brown.

Stir in drained sauerkraut, garlic, bay leaf, paprika, salt, and pepper. Cover and simmer, stirring occasionally for 45 minutes or until sauerkraut is very tender, adding water if necessary.

Serve with rice, pasta or mashed potatoes and bread.

Stuffed cabbage leaves is a dish often prepared for special gatherings and celebrations like weddings and holidays. It is a typical winter dish, but rules are made to be broken. It is simmered on the stovetop and the only rule is: DO NOT STIR. Serve with cooked or mashed potatoes. It is our custom to serve and eat bread with every dish so this one is no exception. If you prefer, you can omit potatoes but why not have both? This recipe is also perfect to portion up and freeze for another time.

Makes 14-18

Ingredients:

1 head of cured/fermented green cabbage*
1 onion, minced
4 tablespoons oil, divided
1lb/500g lean ground beef
1 cup uncooked rice
2 garlic cloves, minced
1 teaspoon paprika
1 tablespoon fresh or dry parsley
1 teaspoon nutmeg
1 teaspoon black pepper
1 teaspoon salt or Vegeta
Water
2 bay leaves
½ lb/250g bacon, smoked rib meat or any other smoked meat
2 tablespoons all-purpose flour
1 tablespoon tomato paste

Directions:

*If your stores don't offer cured cabbage you can substitute it with this quick pickling recipe: Fill half of a large stockpot with water; add 2 cups vinegar, ½ cup of salt and bring to a boil. Carefully place the fresh cabbage head into the hot water and let it cook for about 40 minutes or until cabbage is soft, but not too soft.

Separate each leaf carefully of cured or quickly pickled cabbage head. Rinse, then remove the thick part of the stem without tearing the leaves; set aside. Slice or chop the small or damaged leaves.

In a small saucepan or pan heat 2 tablespoons oil over medium heat. Add onions and sauté until translucent. Transfer onions with oil into a large bowl. Add ground beef, rice, garlic and seasonings; mix well. Place about 2 tablespoons of meat mixture on the edge of each leaf, fold sides to the center and roll away from you. If there is exposed meat, remove some of the filling or wrap another smaller leaf around it. Repeat until meat filling is gone.

Spread the chopped leaves (or sauerkraut) on the bottom of a large pot or Dutch oven. Layer cabbage rolls seam-side down and tight together. Cut the smoked meat into pieces and place on top of the rolls. Spread any leftover cabbage leaves on the top. Add bay leaves and fill with enough water to just cover the rolls. Cover the pot and bring to a boil. Reduce the heat and simmer for about 2 hours, adding more water if necessary.

Heat 2 tablespoons of oil in a small pan. Stir in the flour and mix with a wooden spoon or a whisk over low heat until flour is golden in color. Add tomato paste and mix well. Pour the roux over cabbage rolls and gently press down to dissolve in the juices. Do not stir rolls, as they will disintegrate. Cover the pot and continue to simmer for another hour.

Layers of onion bulbs are used as little holders for meat stuffing in this dish. This is one of the rare dishes I didn't mind helping prepare. We made it a game: who will roll up more onion layers in less time. Don't be put off by onions; they are pre-cooked in vinegar/water mixture to soften and neutralize the flavor before they are stuffed. Open up a rolled onion to find a savory, meaty filling. Serve drizzled with lemon juice and topped with sour cream alongside dense bread.

Makes 18-22

Ingredients:

5-6 large sweet onions (like Vidalia, Walla-Walla or Spanish onions)
Water
¼ cup white vinegar
2lbs/1kg ground beef
1/3 cup rice
1 egg
2 garlic cloves, minced
1 tablespoon tomato paste
1 teaspoon paprika, ground
1 tablespoon salt
½ tablespoon black pepper
2 tablespoons vegetable oil
Sour cream
Lemon juice

Directions:

Peel the onions and cut the ends. Tip: onions of the same size and shape ensure even cooking time. Cut each onion lengthwise stopping half way through. Place onions into a large pot, cover with water and add vinegar. Bring to a boil and cook until soft but not falling apart, about 10 minutes. Remove the onions from the water and let them cool enough for handling.

Combine ground beef, rice, egg, garlic, tomato paste, paprika, salt and pepper in a bowl and mix well with your hands.

Separate layers of onions by gently squeezing out shell after shell. Cover the bottom of a greased large pot with the smallest pieces of onions and reserve some for the top. Fill onion shells with meat mixture, placing a small amount at one end of the shell and then wrapping towards the other end. Repeat until all stuffing is used. Layer filled onions in a pot placing them tightly, one next to the other. Top with some of the remaining small onion layers and add just enough water to cover. Sprinkle with more paprika.
Cover and cook for 45-50 minutes over medium-low heat.

To serve, transfer the stuffed onions onto plates and pour with sauce.

Stuffed peppers give aroma to typically bland zucchini. Zucchini mellows down the strong taste of peppers, creating the flavors that are in perfect harmony. Serve with a dollop of sour cream alongside mashed potatoes or bread.

Serves 4

Ingredients:

3-4 medium green or Hungarian yellow peppers
2 medium zucchini squash (or 4 small)
2 small onions, chopped and divided
1lb/500g lean ground beef
½ cup uncooked rice
1 large garlic clove, diced
½ teaspoon paprika
1 teaspoon salt or Vegeta
1 teaspoon black pepper
1 tablespoon chopped parsley
3 tablespoons Oil, divided
4 cups water
1 tomato, chopped
1 tablespoon all-purpose flour
3 tablespoons tomato paste

Directions:

Wash and de-core the peppers and remove the seeds and membranes. Wash the zucchini. If using medium size zucchini, cut in half. Cut off tops and carefully remove seeds.

In a large bowl, mix one chopped onion, beef, rice, garlic, paprika, salt, pepper, parsley, and one tablespoon oil. Stuff the peppers and zucchini with meat mixture, about 2/3 of the way.

Heat the remaining oil in a large saucepan. Add flour and cook on low heat, stirring constantly until golden brown, about 2-3 minutes. Do not burn. Add chopped onion and tomato; sauté for 5 minutes. Stir in tomato paste. Add water and bring to a boil. Season the sauce with salt and pepper. Place stuffed peppers and zucchini into the boiling sauce; reduce the heat. Cover and simmer for 40-50 minutes or until tender.

TOMATO SOUP – PARADAJZ CORBA

A bowl of hot tomato soup with homemade dumplings is what you need to feel cozy in the cold winter days but it's equally enjoyed all year round. Substitute homemade dumplings with canned butter biscuits. Tear them into quarter size pieces and drop into the boiling soup.

Serves 4

Ingredients:

Soup
2 tablespoons vegetable oil
2 onions, chopped
4 cloves garlic, minced
1 can (28oz/794g) stewed tomatoes
3 cups vegetable or chicken broth
¼ cup tomato paste
½ teaspoon pepper
Fresh basil leaves, chopped
Parmesan cheese, grated

Dumplings
1 egg
¼ cup flour (about)

Directions:

Heat the oil over medium heat in a saucepan. Cook onions and garlic for 5 minutes, stirring frequently.
Add tomatoes, broth, tomato paste and pepper. Bring to a boil then reduce heat and simmer 15 minutes or until slightly thickened.

Puree with an immersion blender or a food blender.

Mix egg with about ¼ cup flour (amount will depend on how firm you like your dumplings) and salt and pepper to taste, until well combined.

Bring soup to just below boiling and drop in dumplings by small spoonfuls. Cook about three minutes, or until dumplings float to the surface.

Serve hot with chopped fresh basil and Parmesan cheese as a garnish if desired.

Main Dishes

BEEF RISSOLES – FASIRANE SNICLE

Soft and juicy, delicious and fragrant, rissoles were loved by our grandmothers and will surely be loved by our grandchildren. Wedge them between bread slices for a hearty sandwich or smother them with gravy of your choice over mashed potatoes, rice or noodles.

Serves 4

Ingredients:

1lb ground beef
1 cup breadcrumbs
1 large egg
1 small onion, chopped
1 garlic clove, minced
1 tablespoon dried parsley
½ teaspoon paprika
1 teaspoon freshly ground black pepper
1 tablespoon salt or Vegeta
4-5 tablespoons all-purpose flour
Oil for frying

Directions:

In a large bowl, using your hand, combine all ingredients except flour and oil. Shape into 4 or 6 round balls and roll each into flour.

In a heavy frying pan, heat the oil over medium-high heat. Place the rissoles in the hot oil. Do not cover. Brown rissoles on both sides then reduce the heat and cook for about 5-10 minutes longer on each side to ensure they are cooked through.

Cevapi [cheh-vah-pee] are finger-sized rolled sausages, highly addictive, classically grilled and served in special pita bread called lepinja or somun with onions, kajmak (cheese), and ajvar (roasted red pepper and eggplant spread). They are commonly made of ground beef, but a mix of equal parts of veal and lamb mince yields the best flavor.

Serves 4-6

Ingredients:

1lb/500g ground beef or veal
1lb/500g ground lamb (or use 2lbs/1kg all beef 80/20 meat/fat ratio)
1 teaspoon salt
½ teaspoon baking soda
½ teaspoon pepper
2 garlic cloves, minced
¼ cup hot water

Directions:

Soak the minced garlic in a little warm water for 10 minutes; drain. Combine all ingredients in a medium bowl. Add more hot water if the mixture feels too dry. Cover the bowl and refrigerate for at least 2 hours or overnight.

Roll a small amount of meat between your palms and shape into sausages, about the size of an index finger. Heat the grill, griddle or grill pan on high. Lay cevapi on the grill making sure not to crowd them. Turn the heat to medium-high and cook cevapi about 4-5 minutes per side, turning once, or until they are a deep brown color and cooked through; remove from grill and keep warm until serving.

If you're serving cevapi with lepinje, slice lepinje in half and spoon with 2 tablespoons of hot broth or water mixed with Vegeta over the insides. Place lepinje face down on the grill and soak up cevapi bits. Spoon more broth over the top and cover with aluminum foil until the broth has steamed away, 2-3 minutes. Remove and fill with cevapi and sliced onions. Serve along ajvar and kajmak (substitute with cream cheese or ricotta cheese).

CHEESE PIE - SIRNICA

Cheese pie or sirnica is a delicious, open face dish made by stuffing phyllo dough with a mixture of cheeses and eggs. Dough made from scratch is always the best option, but a store-bought phyllo dough is fine too when you're in a pinch. This very traditional recipe is versatile by using different stuffing like meat, spinach (add 3-4 cups to this recipe), potatoes, cabbage, zucchini and even apples for a sweet version, giving each pie a different and unique name.

Ingredients:

8 sheets of Phyllo Pastry – jufka, or homemade dough
4 cups Cottage Cheese
1 cup Sour Cream
1 cup Mozzarella Cheese
½ cup Feta Cheese
3 Eggs
1 teaspoon Salt
1 stick Butter, melted

Directions:

Get the pastry to room temperature. This is very important so they don't break as they are very delicate. Once opened, keep them covered with a damp towel.

Preheat your oven to 400F/205C.

In a large bowl beat the eggs. Mix in sour cream, all the cheeses, and salt. On a clean working surface place two sheets of pastry on top of each other. If you're working with the Greek brand, use 4 sheets as they are much thinner.

Lightly brush the melted butter over the top sheet and then spread ¼ of the filling stopping at about 1 inch from the sides. (If you are using homemade dough, spread the cheese mixture evenly all over the stretched out dough and use the same rolling method as in Burek recipe).

Gently start rolling the sheets. You could also place the sheets on a clean tablecloth and lifting the end of it gets the sheets rolled. Spray a little water on the ends so that you can fold them under the rolls. Put the rolls in a greased pan. Repeat this three more times. Use the leftover melted butter and brush over pita rolls, especially all the creases.

Bake in preheated oven for 45 minutes or until golden brown. The thinner sheets need less baking time, around 30 to 35 minutes.

Let it cool before cutting. These taste good cold as well as warm.

CHICKEN BUMP PIE - KVRGUSA

Easy to make, this simple version of chicken pot pie is a traditional Balkan dish made by baking chicken pieces in the batter. The batter will puff up during the baking process creating bumps, hence the name. To serve, top the hot pie generously with sour cream alongside a green, leafy vegetable or salad.

Serves 3-6

Ingredients:

2 eggs
2 ½ cups all-purpose flour
1 tablespoon salt or Vegeta
1 ¼ cup lukewarm water
1 teaspoon black pepper
6 chicken pieces (drumsticks and thighs)
1 cup sour cream
½ cup milk
Oil

Directions:

Preheat oven to 450F/230C.

In a large bowl beat the eggs, flour, salt and water until batter is smooth. Rinse the chicken pieces, brush with oil, and season with salt and pepper.

Lightly grease a large baking pan. Place in the hot oven for a few minutes to warm up (this will prevent the batter from sticking).

Carefully remove the pan from the oven and pour the batter into the pan. Shake the pan lightly to even out the batter. Distribute chicken pieces evenly over the batter.

Return the pan to the oven and bake for 20 minutes. Lower the temperature to 420F/210C and bake until chicken is fully cooked and golden brown, about 20-30 minutes.

Combine sour cream and milk. Spread evenly over the bump pie; bake 5 minutes longer.

CHICKEN PAPRIKASH – PILECI PAPRIKAS

The flavors and colors that inspire happiness are likely those remembered fondly from childhood. The classic chicken paprikash is a popular dish beyond the Balkan region. It is colorful, flavorful and heartwarming. Serve over potatoes, dumplings, rice or pasta.

Serves 3-4

Ingredients:

2-3 tablespoon oil
2 onions, chopped
2 large chicken breasts (legs, thighs, or drumsticks can be used as well)
Salt or Vegeta and black pepper to taste
1 tablespoon sweet paprika, preferably Hungarian
1 small green bell pepper sliced
1 small red bell pepper, sliced
1 clove garlic, minced
1 tablespoon flour
1 cup tomato sauce
1 cup chicken broth
1 tablespoon dried basil
½ teaspoon crushed red pepper flakes
1 tablespoon sour cream

Directions:

Cut chicken into strips. Heat the oil in a large sauté pan over medium-high heat. Add chopped onion and cook, stirring occasionally for 3-4 minutes until translucent.

Place chicken strips in the pan with onions and season with salt, pepper and paprika. Let the chicken cook until done, stirring occasionally so as not to burn the onions, for 20-25 minutes (depending on the size of your chicken pieces) then add peppers and garlic. Cook 10 minutes longer.

Sprinkle the chicken and peppers with flour and stir to combine. Add tomato sauce, broth, basil, and red pepper flakes. Simmer on low heat for 10 minutes or until sauce thickens. Stir in sour cream.

COVERED PORK CHOPS – POKRIVENE KRMENADLE

Nothing says "I love you" like a home-cooked meal. Easy to make but very impressive, this delicious duo is a perfect meal for date night or any other special event. This wonderful pork chop and classy cauliflower meal should be served with a side of mashed potatoes.

Serves 4

Ingredients:

4 pork chops
Salt and ground pepper to taste
3 tablespoons oil
Water
1 cube vegetable bouillon or one tablespoon Vegeta seasoning
4 cups cauliflower florets
4 tablespoons sour cream
1 egg yolk
4 slices Swiss cheese

Directions:

Season pork chops with salt and pepper. Heat the oil in a large skillet over medium heat. Add the pork chops and brown on both sides about 7-10 minutes on each side, depending on their thickness or until done.

Meanwhile, fill a pot with water and bring to a boil. Add the bouillon cube. Clean cauliflower and separate into flowerets. Add to the boiling water, lower the heat and cook for 15 minutes or until tender. Transfer to a colander and let drain well (you can also steam the cauliflower instead).

In a small saucepan add sour cream, egg yolk and a pinch of salt and pepper. Cook sour cream mixture over medium heat whisking continually until the mixture thickens, about 10 minutes.

Remove from heat. Add cooked cauliflower and mash with the fork to a chunky consistency.
In a greased baking pan, place pork chops. Top each pork chop generously with the cauliflower mix and a slice of cheese. Bake in 350F/175C preheated oven until cheese melts, about 10 minutes.

MEATBALLS IN TOMATO SAUCE – CUFTE U PARADAJZ SOSU

Influenced by neighboring Italy, meatballs in tomato sauce are also beloved in Balkan. Ingredients and preparation might slightly vary from region to region. I tried many recipes but my mom's recipe is my favorite to date.

Serves 4-6

Ingredients:

1lb/500g ground beef or pork
1 small onion, chopped and divided
1 clove garlic, minced
1 egg
½ cup breadcrumbs
¼ teaspoon nutmeg
1 tablespoon chopped, fresh parsley
¼ cup lukewarm water
Salt and ground pepper to taste
1 cup all-purpose flour
2 tablespoons oil
1 cup tomato sauce
1 teaspoon tomato paste
1 teaspoon dry oregano
1 teaspoon chopped fresh or dry basil

Directions:

Mix ground beef, half of the onions, garlic, egg, breadcrumbs, nutmeg, parsley, water, salt and pepper in a large bowl by hand until just combined.

Roll meatballs to about the size of a golf ball. Roll each into flour to give it a good coating.

Heat the oil in a large skillet over medium-high. Fry meatballs until just browned, about 3-4 minutes on each side. Don't worry about the center getting cooked through as you will finish these in the sauce.

Remove from the skillet and keep warm. Add 1 tablespoon of flour to the skillet and stir until smooth. Cook until golden yellow. Add remaining chopped onions and sauté until softened. Add tomato sauce, tomato paste, oregano and basil and bring to a low simmer.

Arrange meatballs in the sauce, turning each one over to coat evenly. Cover and simmer gently for 15-20 minutes.

Serve with the sauce over spaghetti or another pasta and crusty bread. Sprinkle with chopped parsley for garnish if you prefer.

MEAT PIE – BUREK

Burek (meat pie) is filled pastry. Here you will learn how to make phyllo dough. You can use store-bought dough but nothing tastes quite like pastry made from scratch. This savory goodness may be prepared in a large pan and cut into portions after baking, or as individual pastries like in this recipe. Serve burek warm or cold with plain yogurt, sour cream or buttermilk.
Serves 4

Ingredients:

Pastry
2 cups all-purpose flour (plus more for dusting)
Salt
2 tablespoon oil, plus more for coating
1 cup warm water

Meat Filling
1 pound ground or finely diced beef or veal (or combination of both)
1 yellow onion, chopped
1 clove garlic, minced
Salt
1 tablespoon black pepper
½ cup hot water

Directions:

In a large bowl, whisk flour and salt to combine. Make a small hole in the middle and add oil and water. Start mixing slowly from the middle out, using your fingers and adding flour from the side of the bowl until mixture forms soft dough that isn't sticky. Note: Depending on air humidity, you might have a little bit of flour left or you might need to add some more. Dough should look similar to pizza dough.

Turn dough onto a floured surface and knead until smooth and pliable. Brush the dough with oil, cover with plastic wrap and set aside to rest for up to an hour at room temperature or store in a refrigerator for up to two days (if refrigerated, allow the dough to reach room temperature).

Combine all ingredients for the meat filling in a small bowl and leave to rest, covered and refrigerated until dough is ready.

Line a large table with a clean tablecloth. Remove the rested dough to a lightly floured work surface. Divide into 4 smaller even pieces. Knead each ball until smooth for about two minutes. Using rolling pin, roll out rounds to a flat circle. Coat each piece with more oil using a pastry brush.

Take one round of dough and place the edge over your floured fists so the rest hangs in the air. One at a time, move your hands up and down to rotate the dough (similar to the way pizza makers do), working your way around the edge of the dough until its weight allows it to stretch into a larger piece. When it's too large to handle, place it on the tablecloth.

Using your fingers, gently shake and pull the edge of the dough towards you to stretch out the center, until it's even and transparent. Size may vary. Trim the thick outer edges and discard.

Drizzle pastry all over with oil. Spread pieces of meat mixture over the pastry. Start to roll the dough on the long side by lifting the tablecloth towards the other side into a long, thin log.

Tightly coil the pita rolls into a swirl. Place into a greased baking dish. Brush the top of the pastry with more oil.

Repeat stretching and rolling the remaining dough and filling. Bake for 35 to 45 minutes in 375F/190C preheated oven until the top and base are crisp and golden. Bring one cup water and one tablespoon butter to a boil and drizzle over pita when done baking.

POLENTA WITH CARAMELIZED ONIONS & PEPPERS – PURA SA LUKOM I PARIKAMA

Polenta is basically a cornmeal mush, except this version is not as mushy. The simplicity of the dish does not compromise the flavor, which varies depending on the topping. Traditionally, there are two basic toppings but let your imagination flow and shake things up with some unexpected pairings. Pura is also very good with buttermilk.

Serves 2

Ingredients:

1 cup yellow coarse cornmeal
3 cups water
1 teaspoon salt
1 tablespoon oil
3 tablespoon butter
1 medium onion, chopped or sliced
1-2 bell peppers (any color), chopped or sliced
1 teaspoon sugar
Salt and pepper to taste
½ cup Feta cheese

Directions:

Mix cornmeal, water, 1 teaspoon salt and oil in a medium size pan. Bring to a light boil over medium-low heat, whisking occasionally.

When polenta starts to bubble, lower the heat to low and whisk frequently, keeping the cornmeal from lumping up and sticking to the bottom of your pan, until desired consistency is reached for about 10 minutes. You want to be able to lift it with the fork, so it should be pretty thick.

Meanwhile, heat the butter in a large skillet. Add onions and peppers and sauté over medium heat until tender, about 5-10 minutes. Add salt, pepper, and sugar and cook until softened, about 5 more minutes.

Scoop the caramelized vegetables over polenta and sprinkle with crumbled feta.

POLENTA WITH SAUERKRAUT AND BACON – PURA SA KISELIM KUPUSOM

After you've tried this polenta you might be inclined to serve it with maple syrup alongside eggs for breakfast, or with milk, sugar, cinnamon, apples, and pecans. Pura is a great side dish to accompany stews. Don't forget to try the version in previous recipe.

Serves 2

Ingredients:

1 cup yellow coarse cornmeal
3 cups water
1 teaspoon salt
1 tablespoon oil
6 bacon strips, sliced
1 cup sauerkraut
½ cup Feta cheese
Black pepper

Directions:

Mix cornmeal, water, 1 teaspoon salt and oil in a medium size pan. Bring to a light boil over medium-low heat, whisking occasionally.

When polenta starts to bubble, lower the heat to low and whisk frequently, keeping the cornmeal from lumping up and sticking to the bottom of your pan, until desired consistency is reached for about 10 minutes. You want to be able to lift it with the fork, so it should be pretty thick.

Meanwhile, heat a skillet over medium heat. Add bacon and sauté until crisp, about 5-8 minutes. Top pura with bacon grease, bacon pieces, sauerkraut, and Feta crumbles. Season it with freshly ground black pepper.

You can add homemade pork crisps/rinds (cvarci) as well if desired.

POTATO AND BEEF CASSEROLE - MUSAKA

Moussaka is to Balkan what lasagna is to Italy: a rich casserole with endless variety, from choices of meat to types of sauce and other ingredients. This simple version of potato and ground beef moussaka gives you an opportunity to hide vegetables for picky eaters. I added a few handfuls of spinach to the meat mixture when it was browned and let it wilt. You can sauté chopped bell pepper with the meat mixture or add a layer of baked eggplant slices for a different flavor.

Serves 6

Ingredients:

4 large potatoes
2 tablespoons cooking oil
1 onion, chopped
1 large carrot, diced
1lb/500g ground beef
1 garlic clove, minced
1 teaspoon paprika
1 tablespoon salt or Vegeta
1 teaspoon black pepper
1/2 cups rice, partially cooked
4 eggs
1 cup milk
¼ cup sour cream

Directions:

Peel the potatoes and slice into thin rounds (about ½-inch or ½-cm). Toss them into lightly salted, boiling water and boil just until they change their color from glossy to matt, about 3-5 minutes. Drain the water.

Meanwhile, heat the oil in a large pan over medium-high heat. Add onions and carrots and sauté until onions are translucent. Add ground beef, garlic, paprika, salt and pepper and brown until no longer pink, about 5-10 minutes. Don't overcook it. Remove from the stove and drain the liquid.

Preheat the oven to 350F/180C. Line the bottom of a greased baking pan with half of the potatoes; evenly spread the meat mixture over the potatoes. Cover with rice and the rest of the potatoes.

In a small bowl, mix eggs, milk, and sour cream; season with salt and pepper to taste. Pour over potatoes and bake 45-60 minutes or until the top layer is a golden brown color. If the top layer starts to brown quickly, cover with foil.

Remove from the oven and let sit for 15-30 minutes before serving. Top with sour cream if desired.

Growing up in the Balkans, lamb was definitely the celebratory roast and it still is. We certainly love our tradition of sitting around a fire, spit-spinning a whole lamb. Just walk down the city river on Labor Day and you'll see rows of roasted lambs accompanied by cheerful families. This most delicious meat can be easily made in your kitchen. Its tenderness and flavor are fit for any celebration. Mix long pasta like spaghetti or fettuccine with roasting juices and serve with crusty bread and salad greens.

Serves 8

Ingredients:

7lbs/ 3kg semi-boneless or boneless leg of lamb
3 large garlic cloves, sliced
Olive Oil
1 tablespoon sea salt
1 teaspoon black pepper
2 tablespoons fresh rosemary, chopped
½ cup light beer

Directions:

Rinse and pat lamb dry. Make incisions all over with the tip of a sharp, small knife. Insert pieces of garlic into incisions. Rub leg with oil, then season with salt, pepper and sprinkle with rosemary. Let stand for 15-30 minutes.

Meanwhile, preheat oven to 375F/190C. Put the lamb into a lightly oiled roasting pan and cover with lid or aluminum foil. Bake, for 2 – 2 ½ hours. Uncover and bake until the surface becomes brown and crisp, about 30 more minutes (internal temperature should be at least 145F/63C for medium-rare and up to 165F/74C for well-done).

Pour beer over roast and return to the oven for 5-10 minutes. Note: beer tends to get bitter the longer it cooks.

Transfer lamb to a platter or carving board; let rest 20 minutes before carving.

STUFFED MEATLOAF – LAZNI ZEC

This mouthwatering meatloaf turns into a festive dish for any occasion when it's stuffed with boiled eggs. Serve warm as a main dish or cold for an appetizer or snack.

Serves 6-8

Ingredients:

1 tablespoon butter
1/3 cup breadcrumbs
1lb/500g lean ground beef
1 egg
1 small onion, finely chopped
2 garlic cloves, minced
2 tablespoons chopped fresh parsley
1 teaspoon paprika
2 teaspoons salt or Vegeta
1 tablespoon freshly ground black pepper
A pinch of nutmeg
1 tablespoon oil
3 hard boiled eggs, peeled
4 slices bacon
2 tablespoons ketchup

Directions:

Preheat oven to 350F/175C. Butter an 8"/20cm loaf pan. Sprinkle the bottom with a tablespoon of breadcrumbs.

In a medium bowl, mix the ground beef, egg, onions, garlic, parsley, paprika, salt, pepper, nutmeg and remaining breadcrumbs with your hand until just combined. Do not overwork it as it will get too tough.
Transfer the mixture to a sheet of plastic wrap or wax paper and pat to form a rectangle.

Place boiled eggs next to each other and using the wrap to start a roll, roll meat over the eggs beginning at the long end. Place seam side down into the loaf pan. Spread top with ketchup. Place bacon slices on top or make a pretty lattice pattern if you desire.

Bake uncovered for about 50 minutes or until bacon is crisp. Let stand 10 minutes. Cut into slices.

Sides

Mlinci is homemade baked pasta. Dried mlinci can be stored in an air-tight container for at least a couple of months. It is rehydrated by boiling in water then drained and tossed with the hot cooking juices of a roasted turkey. This is one of the favorite Christmas and festive dishes. It is easy to prepare and extraordinary in taste.

Serves 8

Ingredients:

2lbs/1kg flour
1½ tablespoons salt
¼ cup duck or pork lard
1 egg
Cold water (about 2 cups)

Directions:

Combine the flour, salt and duck fat in a large mixing bowl. Rub with your fingers until the fat has been worked through the flour. Add the egg and mix it into the flour with your fingers. Add enough cold water to form a firm but soft dough. Knead the dough on a lightly floured surface for five minutes, until soft. Cut the dough into 8 pieces, cover with a tea towel and set aside for at least a half an hour.

Preheat the oven to 350F/170C and set up two racks for baking.

On a lightly floured surface, roll two pieces of the dough to a 2 mm thickness. You don't need to be perfect in what the shape is, only ensuring the rolled out disc will fit on one baking tray. Place the rolled dough onto a flat baking tray or cookie tray, and bake for 10 minutes. Turn the baked dough sheet over and bake further for 8-10 minutes.

Remove the baked dough from the oven and lay on a cooling rack. Repeat the rolling and baking process with the remaining dough balls.

To cook, bring a pot of salted water to the boil. Take 2-4 pieces of the baked dough and snap into 4"/10cm pieces. When the water boils, turn off the heat and drop the pieces of baked dough into the boiled water for about a minute, stirring very gently until they soften. Drain well and put the drained mlinci straight into the hot meat juices. Mix well, but gently, until the juices have coated the mlinci.

Our Balkan grandmothers had numerous incredible and inventive ways to use leftovers and stretch a meal. This satisfying dish is made with stale bread and just a few other ingredients. While baking, its fragrance fills the house with memories of our childhood.

Serves 2-3

Ingredients:

2 cups chicken or vegetable broth
6 slices stale bread or 3 large bread rolls
3 tablespoons butter
1 small onion, chopped
1 teaspoon black pepper
1 tablespoon parsley
1 cup Feta cheese, crumbled
1 egg, beaten
1 pinch nutmeg
1 cup sour cream
Salt to taste

Directions:

Bring broth to a boil in a small saucepan. Cut or tear bread into bite-size pieces. Stir the bread into the broth and set aside until liquid is absorbed. Pour out excess liquid if necessary.

Meanwhile, melt the butter in a small skillet over medium-high heat. Add the onions and sauté until tender, about 10 minutes. Remove from heat and mix with the moist bread. Add pepper, parsley and feta cheese. Gently fold them into the bread mixture. Transfer to a small to medium size baking dish.

In a separate bowl, beat the egg with nutmeg, sour cream and a pinch of salt. (Be careful not to over salt it. Cheese and broth already contain salt!) Pour over the bread mixture and bake on 350F/175C preheated oven for 30 minutes.

Let it sit for 10 minutes before serving.

Chard, a.k.a. Swiss chard or mangold is cooked with potato chunks and seasoned with garlic and olive oil. This simple, delicious and quick side dish is traditionally a great accompaniment to grilled fish but it's wonderful with any meat or alone.

Serves 4-6

Ingredients:

1lb/500g potatoes (like Yukon Gold)
1 large bunch chard (pictured rainbow Swiss chard)
2 garlic cloves, minced
4 tablespoons olive oil
Salt and freshly ground black pepper

Directions:

Bring a large saucepan of salted water and cubed potatoes to a boil.

Meanwhile, rinse the Swiss chard, remove tough stems, and cut into strips. When potatoes are almost done, after about 15 minutes, add the Swiss chard. Cook all together for an additional 10-15 minutes.

In a large skillet, sauté garlic in olive oil over medium heat until it begins to sizzle, about 2 minutes. Add the drained chard and potatoes, season with salt and pepper; stir and cook for 1 more minute to bring all flavors together.

POTATO AND PASTA - GRENADIR

This inexpensive and filling dish can be made by using leftover potatoes and pasta. Balkan cuisine is all about feeding the most people with the least amount of leftovers. Make it a main dish by adding cubed ham or bacon. Serve alongside salad greens.

Serves 3-4

Ingredients:

3 large potatoes
2 cups uncooked pasta (short shaped)
3 tablespoons olive oil
1 onion, chopped
1 tablespoon paprika
Salt and pepper to taste

Directions:

Wash potatoes and cook until tender, about 20 minutes. Drain potatoes and cool until ready to handle. Peel and dice potatoes into bite size chunks. You can also first peel, dice and then cook the potatoes or use leftover mashed potatoes. There's no wrong way.

Meanwhile, in another pot, cook pasta in salted water according to the package directions. Drain pasta and set aside.

In a large skillet, heat the oil over medium-high heat. Add onions and sauté until translucent, about five minutes. Stir in paprika. Add potatoes and pasta and mix to combine. Season it with salt and pepper to taste.

POTATO STUFFED PEPPERS – PAPRIKE PUNJENE KROMPIROM

Vegetables stuffed with various fillings are characteristic of Balkan cuisine. For this dish, the most suitable peppers are sweet Hungarian wax peppers but if you can't find them, any color bell pepper will do the trick. Serve as a side dish or main course.

Serves 4

Ingredients:

4 bell peppers (any color)
3 large potatoes, grated
1 onion, chopped
1 tomato, chopped
1 tablespoon fresh parsley leaves
1 teaspoon freshly ground black pepper
Salt or Vegeta to taste
2 tablespoons oil
Sour cream (optional)

Directions:

Peel and grate potatoes on the big holes of a cheese grater. Rinse the potatoes until water runs clear.
In a large skillet heat the oil over medium heat. Add onions and sauté until translucent. Add tomatoes and potatoes and cook, stirring occasionally until potatoes are softened but not cooked through, about 5 minutes.

Preheat oven to 375F/190C.

Cut a thin slice from stem end of each bell pepper to remove the top of pepper. Remove seeds and membranes; rinse peppers. Fill each pepper with potato mixture. Place stuffed peppers in a greased baking dish and cover tightly with aluminum foil. Bake for 15 minutes then remove the foil and continue baking for another 40-50 minutes or until potatoes are done.

Spread a tablespoon of sour cream, if using, on top of each pepper and return to the oven for 5-10 minutes longer.

ice with vegetables is another tasty meal originating from the Balkan region that is served
s a side dish or main course. To turn it into a main dish, brown the chicken or beef pieces
efore adding the rice and simmer until meat is cooked through.

erves 4

ngredients:

tablespoons oil
cup chopped onion
cup chopped bell pepper
medium carrot, chopped
cloves garlic, minced
tomatoes
cup uncooked rice
cup frozen or fresh peas
teaspoon paprika
teaspoon chili powder, optional
cups vegetable or chicken broth
alt and pepper to taste
resh parsley leaves

Directions:

n a medium size pan, heat the oil over medium-high heat. Sauté onion, pepper and carrot
ntil softened, about 3 minutes. Add garlic and chopped tomatoes and, stirring frequently,
ook for 5 more minutes.

Mix in the rice, peas, paprika and chili powder, if using. If you like it spicy, adjust the
mount of chili powder.

Add broth and bring to boil. Lower the heat, cover and cook until liquid is absorbed, about
0 to 15 minutes, stirring occasionally. Add salt and pepper to taste.
Sprinkle with chopped parsley leaves.

Salads

BEET SALAD – SALATA OD CIKLE

Beets are not only delicious but packed with healthy nutrients. If you're not a big fan of beets, shred them and mix with salad greens and other salad fixings. This simple, garlicky salad lets the earthy and sweet beet flavor truly shine. Use jarred beets for a shortcut. My 4-yro granddaughter is known to eat this salad by the handful.

Serves 2

Ingredients:

2 medium fresh beets
1 tablespoon oil
2 tablespoons white vinegar
1 garlic clove, minced
Salt and freshly ground black pepper to taste

Directions:

Snip off the greens from the beets, if attached, and leave the "tails" on (prevents the pigment from leaking). You can cook the greens separate like you would Swiss chard, or just discard them.

In a large saucepan bring about 4 cups of water to a boil. Place the beets into boiling water and cook for 40 minutes; drain and cool. Peel the skin using disposable gloves to prevent staining of your hands.

Slice the beets or cut into chunks. Drizzle with oil, vinegar, and garlic. Season the salad with salt and pepper. Enjoy.

CABBAGE SALAD – KUPUS SALATA

Shredded cabbage marinated with oil and vinegar is commonly served as a side in many traditional meals all across the Balkans. Other variations include the addition of tomatoes, peppers, and onions. This salad is my daughter's favorite salad ever since she was a wee child. She preferred salad over candy any day.

Serves 2-4

Ingredients:

1 small head of green cabbage (or 350g/12oz bag shredded cabbage)
1 teaspoon salt
1 garlic clove, minced
¼ teaspoon black pepper
1 tablespoon oil
2 tablespoons white vinegar

Directions:

Core and thinly shred the cabbage; place in a bowl. Sprinkle with salt and mix well. Let cabbage sit for about 20 minutes. With your hand, squeeze the cabbage to discard the liquid.

Add garlic, pepper, oil and vinegar and toss gently to combine. Season with more salt if necessary.

COTTAGE CHEESE SALAD – SIRILUK

This cheese salad accompanies all barbecues and picnics. It has been a loyal member of traditional table spreads for ages. Originally, fresh cow cheese is used for this recipe mixed with sour cream to smooth out the texture. It takes about a whip to make it.

Ingredients:

16oz/500g small curd cottage cheese
¼ cup chopped green onion
1 teaspoon vegetable oil
Salt and pepper to taste

Directions:

Combine all ingredients and refrigerate before serving.

Velvety soft lettuce forms the basis for this simple and tasty salad. It's a great way to add green to your menus and is so refreshing. Adding cooked beef is optional but highly recommended. Every time I cook beef soup I must accompany it with this salad. Tender beef from the soup rounds up this salad to perfection.

Ingredients:

1 head Boston lettuce (or use Bibb or Butter lettuce)
2 hard boiled eggs, sliced
2 green onions, white and green part, sliced
½ pound cooked beef or roast beef, (optional)
1 tablespoon oil
2 tablespoons lemon juice (or white vinegar)
Salt and freshly ground black pepper to taste

Directions:

Separate the lettuce leaves. Tear the larger, outer leaves in half; wash and rinse the lettuce. Put the lettuce leaves in a large serving bowl.

Whisk together oil, lemon juice, salt, and pepper; drizzle over the lettuce.

Add eggs, onions, and chopped beef if using; toss well. Serve immediately.

POTATO SALAD – KROMPIR SALATA

This potato salad is low budget approved. Tangy vinegar and onions complement the soft potato texture. It can be served warm or cold. I prefer it cold during hot summer months. I love the simplicity of this salad and if I'm not careful I could eat a whole bowl in one sitting. It is best accompanied with fish.

Serves 4

Ingredients:

1lb/500g potatoes, unpeeled
1 small onion, thinly sliced
½ teaspoon salt
¼ teaspoon black pepper
2 tablespoons oil
2 tablespoons white vinegar

Directions:

Cook unpeeled potatoes in a pot of boiling water until tender, about 20-30 minutes (depending on the size of potatoes); drain. Let sit until cool enough to handle, about 10-15 minutes. Peel potatoes and cut into slices.

Place potatoes in a large bowl. Add onions, salt, pepper, oil, and vinegar. Gently toss to coat. Serve immediately or cool to room temperature.

ROASTED RED PEPPER SALAD – SALATA OD PECENIH PAPRIKA

Preserving the harvest for winter by pickling and jarring was a must for every household. With fresh produce available throughout the year, making this garlicky salad is now a breeze. It stores well in the refrigerator in an airtight container for up to a week.

Serves 4

Ingredients:

2 large red bell peppers
1-2 garlic cloves, minced
1-2 tablespoons olive oil
1 tablespoons vinegar
Salt and pepper to taste

Directions:

Heat the oven to 500F/260C.

Place peppers on a piece of foil and put on the highest rack. Bake 15 minutes on each side. The skin will start to peel, and blacken in places. If you notice too much blackening, lower the temperature a little bit so the peppers don't burn.

After 30 minutes, take out and let cool. Peel the skin off. Cut each pepper in fours lengthwise, and clean the seeds out.

Keep in the fridge for an hour. Take out, sprinkle with minced garlic, olive oil, and vinegar. Add salt and pepper to taste.

Made for holidays and parties, this salad resembles a potato salad but it tastes unlike any potato salad I've ever had. We intermittently call it a Russian or French salad. Don't ask why, because I don't know. All I know is that it tastes amazing. You can peel and dice potatoes and carrots before cooking them, or do it after they're cooked. Either way is fine.

Ingredients:

2 large potatoes
2 large carrots, peeled
1 cup cooked sweet peas (can use canned)
½ cup chopped dill pickles
3 hard-boiled eggs, chopped
1 cup diced ham or bologna
1 cup mayonnaise
1 tablespoon sour cream
Salt and pepper to taste

Directions:

Cook potatoes and carrots separately in small saucepans with lightly salted water until fork tender but not overcooked. Cooking time depends on their size. Cool completely then peel the potatoes. Dice carrots and potatoes if you haven't done so before cooking.

In a large bowl, gently combine all ingredients. Cover and chill in the refrigerator before serving.

Desserts

I was never much of a baker as I don't like measuring ingredients. Desserts like baklava intimidated me until recently when I finally challenged myself to try my hand at making it. I found it is actually pretty easy to put together. Flaky, crisp and tender layers of phyllo separated with melted butter and filled with nuts make baklava, a traditional treat enjoyed at celebrations throughout the year.

Ingredients:

4 cups sugar + 2 tablespoons
3 cups water
1 lemon, sliced
1 lb/500g walnuts
1 teaspoon ground cinnamon
1 package (16oz/500g) Phyllo dough - pastry leaves (thawed if frozen)
4 sticks of unsalted butter (about 250g)

Directions:

In a medium saucepan, combine 4 cups sugar, lemon slices, and water; bring to a boil. Reduce heat and simmer until sugar dissolves and the mixture is syrupy, about 10-15 minutes. See aside to cool.

In a food processor, pulse walnuts until finely ground. You can also use a rotary grater if you have one. In a large bowl, combine walnuts with cinnamon and remaining two tablespoons of sugar.

Unroll phyllo dough. Cut the whole stack, if necessary, to fit the pan. (I mostly use 13x9-inch/33x23-cm pan). Cover phyllo with a clean cloth to keep from drying out as you work.

Preheat oven to 350F/180C. Butter the bottom and sides of a pan. Place 1 sheet of dough in prepared baking pan; using a pastry brush, butter thoroughly. Repeat with two more sheets of phyllo, laying each on top of the other. Sprinkle with 1/3 cup of walnut filling. Repeat until filling or dough is used up, finishing with the phyllo dough on top.

Using a sharp knife cut the unbaked baklava into squares or diamonds all the way to the bottom of the pan. Pour remaining butter over the whole baklava and lightly sprinkle the top of pastry with cold water. This inhibits the pastry from curling.

Bake baklava for 50-60 minutes or until golden and crisp. Remove from the oven and immediately spoon syrup over it. Let cool for at least 4 hours.

Plum dumplings are common dessert throughout the Balkans whenever plums are plentiful. Small plums are preferable but you can use pieces of regular plums if necessary. If you prefer, add a small cube of sugar into each plum or even a shot of rum or rum extract. For a different texture substitute half of the flour with cream of wheat.

Makes 8

Ingredients:

2 large potatoes, peeled and boiled
1 tablespoon butter
1 egg
¼ teaspoon salt
1 to 1 ½ cups all-purpose flour
8 Italian prune plums, pitted or 2 large plums (like Black Beauty) pitted and quartered
1/3 cup vegetable oil
1/3 cup plain bread crumbs
1 cup sugar
1 teaspoon cinnamon
Sour cream (optional)

Directions:

In a medium bowl, mash potatoes with salt and butter; let cool. Add egg and mix until well combined. Add flour and knead until soft dough forms.

With lightly floured hands, take a portion of dough and pat it flat. Place a plum in the center and bring sides of dough over plum, enclosing it completely. Moisten hands if necessary.

In a large pot, bring salted water to a boil. Lower the heat to medium. One at a time put dumplings into boiling water. Cook for 10-15 minutes. Dumplings are done when they rise to the top.

In a large pan, heat oil over medium heat; add bread crumbs. Stir for a couple of minutes or until they darken just a bit. Using a slotted spoon, add cooked dumplings to the breadcrumbs and roll them in the pan to coat completely. Transfer to a plate.

In a small bowl combine the sugar and cinnamon.

Serve dumplings topped with a dollop of sour cream and sprinkled with sugar/cinnamon mixture.

RICE PORRIDGE – SUTLIJAS

Sutlijas is a simple breakfast or dessert dish made from rice and milk and traditionally topped with cinnamon and raisins, but let your imagination flow.

Serves 4

Ingredients:

½ cup medium-grain rice
1 cup water
A pinch of salt
2 cups coconut milk (or regular)
1 tablespoon vanilla extract
1-2 tablespoons brown sugar

Choices of toppings:
Cinnamon, nutmeg, honey, nuts (peanuts, walnuts, and pistachios) diced dates, raisins, coconut flakes, grated chocolate, fruit.

Directions:

In a medium saucepan, combine rice, water, and salt. Bring to a gentle boil; cover the pan, reduce the heat to low and simmer until liquid is absorbed, about 10-15 minutes.

Add milk, vanilla, and sugar and continue simmering, stirring occasionally, until creamy, about 15-20 minutes.

Note: cook longer if the pudding is too runny and add more milk if it's too thick. Keep in mind, as it cools down, it will become more solid so you want that creamy consistency when you take it off the stove.

Serve warm or cold and garnished with your favorite toppings.

These simple cookies require few ingredients, but the end product is unbeatable. They are rolled in very original way, over a grater, to give them their unusual appearance. Add coconut flour into the mixture for an unforgettable flavor.

Makes 20-30

Ingredients:

Cookies
2 eggs
½ cup sugar
Zest of 1 lemon
½ cup oil
2 ½ cups all-purpose flour (substitute 1 cup flour with 1 cup coconut flour)
1 tablespoons baking powder
Walnut halves/pieces

Syrup
2 cups water
2 cups sugar
Juice of 1 lemon

Directions:

In a bowl, combine eggs, sugar, lemon zest and oil. Add flour and baking powder and knead until soft, smooth dough is formed that does not stick to your hands (add more flour if necessary).

Divide dough into equal parts; flatten in your hand, put a piece of walnut in the middle and close (I make mine the size and thickness of my index finger – they will rise and spread a little during baking).

Press each piece of dough over a grater, flattening them a bit, to form a pattern. Place the cookies on an ungreased baking sheet and bake in a 350F/180C preheated oven until golden, about 20-30 minutes.

Meanwhile, dissolve sugar in water and lemon juice. Ladle syrup over hot cookies; set aside until the cookies soak up all the syrup. Best if made a day ahead. Keep refrigerated.

ROASTED MIXED FRUIT – PECENO MJESANO VOCE

This warm dessert is best served over ice cream. Oven roasted until softened then drizzled with cinnamon caramel sauce and nuts, this dish of mixed fruit yields soft and crunchy goodness. Use any fruit in season.

Serves 6

Ingredients:

1-2 peaches or nectarines
1 large pear
4-5 Italian prune plums (or 2 regular black plums)
4-5 fresh figs
1 cup blueberries
Juice of ½ a lemon
1 tablespoon sugar
1-2 whole cloves (optional)
2 tablespoons butter
3 tablespoons honey
1 teaspoon cinnamon
A pinch of nutmeg
3 tablespoons pistachio, chopped
3 tablespoons walnuts, chopped
2 tablespoons pine nuts, or chopped hazelnuts
 tablespoon Vanilla sugar (or regular sugar + 1 teaspoon Vanilla extract)

Directions:

Preheat oven to 350F/175C

Wash the fruit, remove pits and cut into halves or quarters. Score an x into figs. Place the fruit on an 8"/20cm baking dish arranging plums and figs upright. Sprinkle with lemon juice and sugar if the fruit is not quite ripe. Add cloves and bake for 10-15 minutes.

Meanwhile, melt the butter in a small saucepan over medium heat. Add honey, cinnamon and nutmeg. Lower the heat and simmer, stirring until the sauce thickens into caramel consistency. Pour over baked fruit, top with nuts and vanilla sugar and bake additional 5 minutes.

Serve warm with ice cream or alone.

Poached walnut-stuffed apples have the flavor of apple pie without making the crust. It is a simple and inexpensive classic recipe that comes together quickly.

Serves 6

Ingredients:

6 medium size apples (like Golden Delicious)
2 tablespoons lemon juice
2-4 cups water
2 cups sugar
1 cup ground walnuts
¼ teaspoon cinnamon
1 package vanilla sugar (substitute with 1 tsp sugar and 1 tsp vanilla extract)
2 tablespoons hot milk
Whipped cream and brandied cherries for garnish

Directions:

Peel and core apples. In a saucepan large enough to hold all the apples, mix together sugar, lemon juice and enough water to cover the apples.

Place apples in the pan. Cook on medium heat until tender but still firm, about 10-15 minutes. With a slotted spoon, carefully remove apples from the water and leave them on a rack to cool. Reserve the poaching liquid.

Mix ground walnuts, cinnamon, and vanilla sugar with hot milk until smooth. Fill the cooled apples with this mixture.

Serve chilled or at room temperature. Pour reserved poaching liquid over the apples and top with whipped cream. Garnish with brandied or candied cherries if desired.

Tip: ground walnuts in a food processor.

The Larder

Bread is a staple in Balkan cuisine and is served with every meal. Baking bread from scratch will satisfy all of your senses and make your family happy. Try it and you will never look back. I use different recipes and methods but this one is the most basic and one of my favorites. The crust is crispy but the inside is soft.

Ingredients:

1 ½ teaspoons yeast, active-dry
1 ¾ cups lukewarm water
3 ½ cups unbleached, all-purpose flour, more for dusting
2 teaspoons salt
1 tablespoon coarse cornmeal (optional)

Directions:

In a large bowl, dissolve yeast and salt in water. Stir in flour, mixing until there are no dry patches. Dough will be loose. Cover with a towel; let the dough rise at room temperature for at least 2 hours and up to 5 hours if refrigerated.

Punch down dough. Turn dough in hands to lightly stretch surface, creating a rounded top and a lumpy bottom. Stretch rounded dough into an oval and place in a greased, cornmeal – dusted, nonstick loaf pan. Dust top with one tablespoon flour. Cover pan with plastic wrap; let rest 40 minutes if fresh and an extra hour if previously refrigerated.

Preheat oven to 450F/230C.

Using a serrated or very sharp knife, make a slash across the top of the loaf. Cover pan tightly with foil. Bake on lowest oven rack for 25 minutes.

Reduce oven setting to 400F/200C. Remove foil; bake bread 25-30 minutes longer or until deep golden brown. Bake less if your oven tends to be really hot. Always keep your eye on it as oven temperatures vary. Remove loaf to a wire rack to cool. Let completely cool before slicing.

There's nothing quite like the mesmerizing smell of freshly roasted coffee beans. Brewing coffee is almost a ritual – hot water is poured over fresh, unfiltered, pulverized grounds and served from djezva (narrow-necked pot with a long handle) in a fildzan (small, handle-less coffee cup). Quickly dip the corner of a sugar cube into your coffee, nibble it, and then let the coffee wash it down.

Serves 2

Ingredients:

1 cup water
2 teaspoons finely ground coffee
Sugar cubes (optional)

Directions:

In a small saucepan bring water to a boil.

Place the coffee into a djezva and heat over moderate heat for 30 seconds to warm up, stirring constantly. Pour half of the water over coffee and simmer, allowing the liquid to rise to the point of overflowing and create thick foam. Repeat the process by adding the remainder of the water.

Lepinja or somun is the daily bread of the Balkans best known for housing cevapi, garlicy veal & lamb sausages, a popular street food. Lepinja is pita-like flatbread, tender and spongy. Fill lepinja with rich, savory cream cheese (kajmak) and put it on the grill or under a broiler for a few minutes and you will easily get addicted to this treat.

Makes 6-8

Ingredients:

2 packages active dry yeast
1 tablespoon sugar
¾ cup lukewarm water
8 cups all-purpose flour
1 tablespoon salt
2 cups milk at room temperature

Directions:

Combine yeast, 1 tablespoon flour, sugar, and water in a small bowl. Set aside until it starts to rise and bubble up, about 10-15 minutes.

In a large bowl, whisk together remaining flour and salt. Add yeast mixture and slowly adding milk, mix or knead well by hand until soft dough forms, about 7 minutes. The dough will be somewhat sticky. Cover with plastic wrap and a kitchen towel and let rise in warm place until it doubles in size, at least 1 hour.

Transfer dough to a generously floured surface and divide into 6 to 8 equal portions. With a palm of your hand, form portions into balls, cover and allow them to rest for 10-15 minutes flatten them with your hands or a rolling pin into about a ½ -inch/1cm. Transfer to a parchment paper cut the size of your baking pan. Let the floured dough rounds rest for another 20-30 minutes. With the dull side of a knife, lightly press a crisscross pattern into the dough (optional).

With the baking pan inside, preheat the oven to its maximum temperature (usually 500F/260C). Carefully remove the pan from the oven; place the dough rounds with parchment paper on the pan and return to the oven; bake 7-15 minutes (depending on their size) or until golden.

Remove from the oven, cover with a clean dishtowel and let rest for 10 minutes before slicing. You can freeze lepinje for up to six months.

Ajvar, roasted pepper and eggplant relish, is my favorite among all the jar-packed goodies that were prepared for the winter in our household. Its smoky, garlicky flavor is a perfect match for grilled meats, especially cevapi – skinless sausage links. It is also greatly enjoyed as a quick snack, spread on a thick slice of bread. Like all good food it takes time to prep and cook, but the final outcome is definitely worth it.

Makes about 4 jars

Ingredients:

11lbs/5kg red bell peppers
5 ½ lb/2 ½ kg eggplant
4 cups oil
2-3 garlic cloves, minced
2 tablespoons white vinegar
2-3 tablespoons salt
1 teaspoon black pepper

Directions:

Preheat oven to 475F/246C.

Place the peppers on the baking sheet and roast in the oven, turning occasionally, until the skin is blackened on all sides and the peppers are softened, about 20-30 minutes. Place in a large bowl and let sit, covered, until cool enough to handle.

Meanwhile, place the eggplant, cut-side down, on a lightly oiled baking sheet and roast until soft and skin is charred, about 20-30 minutes. Remove to another large bowl and cover to steam.

Remove the seeds, stems and peels from peppers and eggplant. It's ok if you leave some, don't get nit-picky. To cut down on cooking time, let peppers and eggplant sit in a colander for at least 8 hours to drain the excess liquid. In a food processor, finely chop together peppers, eggplant pulp and garlic (do in batches if necessary).

Heat the oil in a large stockpot. Add chopped peppers and eggplant; bring to a boil over medium-high heat. Reduce the heat to medium-low and simmer, stirring frequently with a wooden spoon, until relish is thick enough to leave a trace when you move across with the spoon, about 1-2 hours. Add salt, pepper, and vinegar and cook 5 minutes longer.

Note: for a spicy relish, add whole jalapeno or chili peppers during the cooking time then remove when the desired level of heat is reached.

Fill the clean jars with ajvar and place uncovered into a 160F/70C preheated oven for about 1 ½ hours. Turn the oven off and leave the jars in to cool overnight or for about 12 hours. Top each jar with a tablespoon of oil and close with a lid.
Store in a cool, dark pantry or in a refrigerator.

Slaughtering pigs for winter to produce smoked ham, ribs, homemade sausages, and bacon is a Balkan tradition held for countless decades. The rendered fat is used for cooking or simply spread on bread with a sprinkle of salt & paprika powder, and the crunchy remnants – cvarci – are seasoned and boxed up in the fridge for a snack. Very little is wasted. Making this in your kitchen is easy, but you'll need to keep your windows open.

Ingredients:

4lbs/2kg pork back bacon with mostly fat, diced into ½"/1cm pieces
1 teaspoon milk
Salt, to taste
Smoked paprika, to taste

Directions:

Put the diced fat into a large saucepan over medium-low heat. Higher heat will result in discoloring your fat and probably burn it. Do not cover the pan – condensed water vapor will cause grease to splatter.

Simmer over low heat, with frequent stirring, until cvarci float to the surface, about 1 to 1 ½ hours.
Chunks of fat will reduce in size and take on a light yellow-golden color. Continue rendering for 10-15 minutes longer until the chunks turn a little crispy and golden. Add milk and immediately turn off the heat. Stir for a couple of minutes then strain the fat through a fine sieve into a bowl and cool down to room temperature. Makes about 4 cups.

Pour rendered fat into very clean and dry jars with lids. Store jars in the refrigerator for several months.

Lightly press pork rinds with a potato masher - just enough to squeeze the excess fat. Sprinkle the rinds with paprika then let cool. Salt the rinds right before serving because with time, the salt will draw the liquid out of them and they will become tough. Store them in the refrigerator, in an airtight container. Yields about 3 cups.

\###

Thank you for reading my book. If you enjoyed it, won't you please take a moment to leave me a review at your favorite retailer? Thanks!
Jas

Connect with me:
Friend me on Facebook: https://www.facebook.com/AllThatsJas/
Subscribe to my blog: http://all-thats-jas.com/
Follow me on Twitter: https://twitter.com/all_thats_jas

Printed by CreateSpace

Made in the USA
San Bernardino, CA
10 November 2018